AF305224

'Bonsoir'

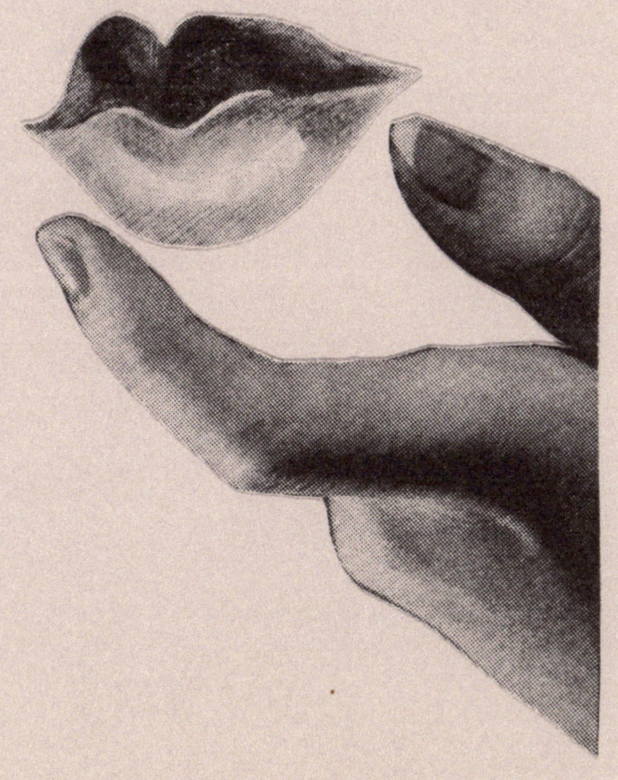

Ithell Colquhoun

Introduction
Amy Hale

It has taken several decades since her death for the world to start to apprehend the multifaceted brilliance that is Ithell Colquhoun. She was a force of nature: a prolific artist, essayist, novelist and poet whose overriding concerns were with spiritual transcendence and union with the divine energy that animated all matter. For her, surrealism, the artistic affiliation she fiercely asserted for most of her life, provided a method and framework with which to explore the deepest reaches of her own mind and connect with other beings and dimensions. We are witnessing a coalescing of interests that is thrusting Colquhoun's oeuvre into the spotlight: a renewed appreciation of surrealism, a new critical commitment to amplifying the historical contribution of women artists, and — crucially — growing interest in esoterically motivated art. This cultural moment is truly Colquhoun's perfect storm.

Born in 1906 in India into a family with a long history of Indian colonial administration, Colquhoun always felt a sense of cultural and spiritual displacement. It is no wonder that she gravitated towards an art movement that placed liminality at the centre of the artistic process. Her childhood in England was unconventional, and her artistic talents were evident from an early age. Her education focused on art and design, paralleled by a growing interest in the occult. Eventually she received a degree from the Slade School of Art in 1930 while participating in London's heady occult community, primarily through her involvement with G.R.S. Mead's Quest Society.[1] After earning her degree, she spent several years travelling, drawing and painting in the Mediterranean. Her first major solo show was in Cheltenham in 1936, the year that she also attended the International Surrealist Exhibition in London — an event that changed her life.

Colquhoun and British surrealism

It was not until three years after her introduction to the British surrealist community that Colquhoun entered the scene with full force. The June 1939 edition of *The London Bulletin* felt like an artistic arrival, featuring two of Colquhoun's prose poems, the announcement of her show at the Mayor Gallery, which was held adjacent to an exhibition by leading British surrealist Roland Penrose, and a short essay, 'What Do I Need to Paint a Picture?', accompanied by an odd assortment of images of Colquhoun painting and sunbathing topless. Although 1939 was a critical year in terms of her recognition within the wider community of surrealism, compared to her later efforts it was a rather tepid outing. She was still finding her feet and voice as a surrealist, and *Bonsoir* was likely part of this process.

Colquhoun's official relationship with the British surrealists was short lived. In 1940, E.L.T. Mesens, the Belgian surrealist promoter, gallery owner and organiser of the British surrealists, had recognised the need to fortify a crumbling art movement that was being shredded by the pressures of the Second World War. He gathered the surrealists together and laid down his rules for continued engagement. Colquhoun, who was deeply invested in her own autonomy, refused to get on board with Mesens' programme. Although it is often reported that Colquhoun was asked to leave because of her occult interests, in reality Colquhoun was the one who left. Although he was not as attracted to occult themes as André Breton, the other leading light of surrealism, it was Mesens' insistence that the British surrealists devote themselves exclusively to the movement, at the expense of all other groups or publishing efforts, that Colquhoun could not accept. Mesens also demanded political allegiance to a revolutionary proletariat agenda, a political commitment that Colquhoun felt was stifling to her vision as an artist. Colquhoun knew her own mind and had forceful interests. She would not be contained. Yet in the years after her official separation from the movement, she produced some of her strongest surrealist work.

For Colquhoun, surrealism was a way of life and an approach to interacting with the world that exceeded the boundaries and restrictions of community. She was deeply interested in surrealist methods and themes, regardless of her official relationship with the wider surrealist milieu. She considered herself to be a lifelong surrealist and continued to experiment with the automatic methods typical of the movement until her final years. In 1943, she married the charismatic renegade surrealist Toni del Renzio, and together they attempted to wrest back surrealism from what they considered to be ideologically corrupt influences. Colquhoun continued to champion the idea of an orthodox Bretonian surrealism, one based on the exploration of the subconscious, liberty and automatism. Even prior to her landmark 1949 essay 'The Mantic Stain', in which Colquhoun outlined the importance of automatism, methods emphasising chance and the unconscious were the crux of her surrealist practice, which was indelibly tied to occult principles and aesthetics. Yet her attempts with del Renzio to revive a true surrealist movement were met with open hostility and aggressive retaliation by the other surrealists, and the two failed to find an audience. By 1947 Colquhoun's marriage was over. Shunned by the British surrealists, yet still faithful to the cause, she moved her artistic production to Cornwall, where she focused on new contexts for surrealism and automatism in her writing and her magic.

Situating *Bonsoir*

Bonsoir was made in 1939, at the height of Colquhoun's public engagement with British surrealism. Colquhoun never gravitated towards film or photography with any sort of sustained artistic interest, and this project is an outlier in her corpus. Yet it is possible that this project was a nod to the defining surrealist film efforts of the period (see Matthew Gale's afterword, p.55), particularly the black-and-white collaborations of Salvador Dalí and Luis Buñuel: *Un Chien Andalou* ('An Andalusian dog') 1929 and *L'Age d'Or* ('The Golden Age') 1930. *Bonsoir* shares with the latter scenes of excess and opulence, 'deviant' sexuality and strange, possibly metaphorical, cameos by animals. While it cannot be conclusively demonstrated that *Bonsoir* was in any way a commentary on *L'Age d'Or*, Colquhoun took great issue with the surrealists' regard for the Marquis de Sade as a figurehead of liberty. The final scene of the film, which takes place after a de Sade-style orgy in a castle in which women have been the victims of men's lust, would have left Colquhoun quite cold, to put it mildly. In this context, *Bonsoir* as a surrealist filmic enterprise becomes a reprioritisation of women's desire.

Despite her apparent lack of interest in film, Colquhoun was interested in collage, cut-ups[2] and found objects. *Bonsoir* is unusual in that it was an early embrace of collage for Colquhoun. She recognised collage's role within surrealist artistic production, eventually writing about the practice in 'The Mantic Stain', yet only adopted it in her own practice more vigorously later in her career. Colquhoun greatly admired the work of Kurt Schwitters and, starting in the 1960s, emulated his methods with a focus on creating Merz[3] collages. She continued collage and cut-up work until quite late in her life. Of course, collage was also a magical practice for Colquhoun. She believed that collage had roots in contemporary occultism, and argued that occult artists such as Moina Mathers were using it before its discovery by surrealists.

Colquhoun was interested in the idea of found imagery, a technique she used more frequently in her poetry and writing than in her visual art. She enjoyed taking images out of their original context to create a new narrative. She would take texts from tables of contents or other lists and repurpose them as poetry, reframing them in entirely different contexts. She believed that this activity had a mantic quality, as the subconscious could illuminate multiple meanings in a given text.

Bonsoir the story

Although *Bonsoir* was labelled as a storyboard, it seems incomplete as a film project because there are no accompanying directorial directions. It is possible that the project did not advance beyond its early stages, or that it was intended to reference the process of storyboarding while constructing a narrative through collage and found image. What can we make of this story?

In many ways, despite employing surrealist techniques, *Bonsoir* is not a particularly surreal tale. It does not rely on strange dream imagery or jarring visual juxtapositions. The tale of *Bonsoir* is that of an upscale couple having a boozy night out on the town with an unexpected erotic development. After what seems like a number of drinks, the woman of the couple turns her attention to another woman, and appears to leave her male partner to engage in a sapphic sexual liaison. When the tryst is discovered by the male partner, there is a struggle and perhaps even a poisoning of some sort, but it is unclear exactly what the outcome of this struggle is. *Bonsoir* explores themes that Colquhoun found interesting and personally relevant, even if not particularly 'surreal'. Of course, a lesbian affair would have been regarded as 'deviant' within the wider context of surrealist commentary on sexuality. The repetition of the lipstick motif is consistent with Colquhoun's emphasis on iconography associated with the feminine, which in many ways was her symbolic wheelhouse, used here almost like punctuation to signify bold, explicitly feminine sensuality.

Biographically, the plot twist is a significant one, likely an exploration of Colquhoun's own grappling with her sexual and gender identity. In 1933, during a trip to Greece, she fell in love with a woman named Andromache or 'Kyria' Kazou. Colquhoun asked Kazou to come and live with her in London, but her offer was refused. Although it is not yet known if she had other same-sex romantic relationships, her artistic circle in Cornwall included lesbians and queer artists such as Gluck and Marlow Moss. Colquhoun's work in the 1940s only occasionally included same-sex erotica, but many of her well-known surrealist pieces were thinly veiled explicit explorations of women's bodies and fleshy feminine sensuality disguised as caves, flowers and trees. Perhaps in this instance the surrealist interest in deviance provided a useful framework for Colquhoun to explore her own desire.

The final frame of *Bonsoir* may well be the most surreal of all the images: a seemingly displaced image of three black cats. Is this the 'reveal' of the story? What do the cats tell us about the nature and inclinations of the actors involved? Was the story about them all along; are they voyeurs? Perhaps they are shapeshifters after an eventful night, renewed and ready to carouse again. This ambiguous ending leaves the audience wondering what Colquhoun meant by the title, *Bonsoir*, as perhaps a 'good evening' was had after all.

'Bonsoir'

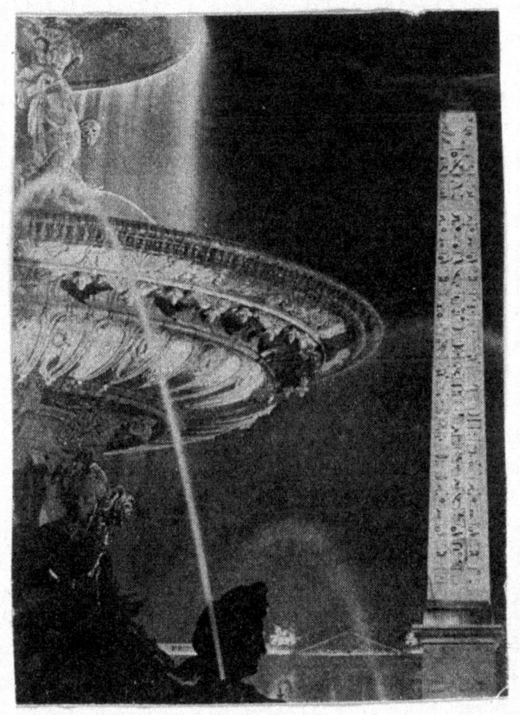

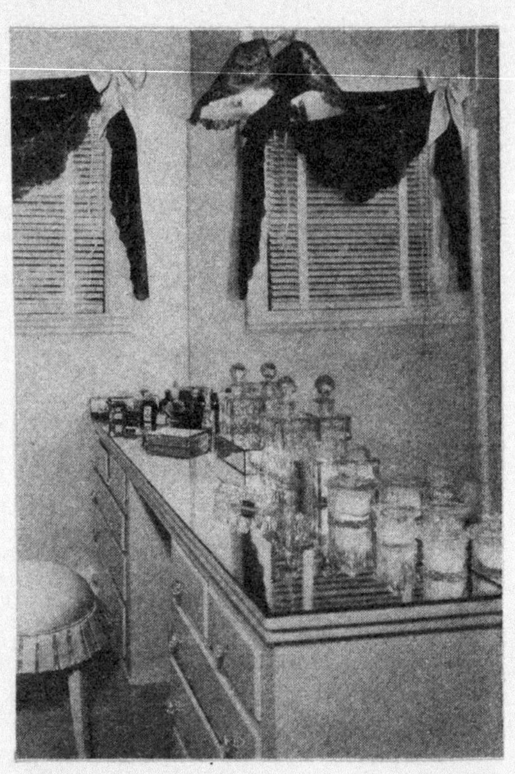

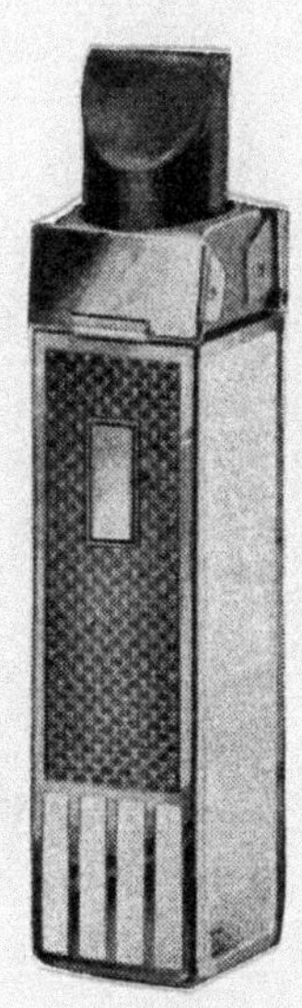

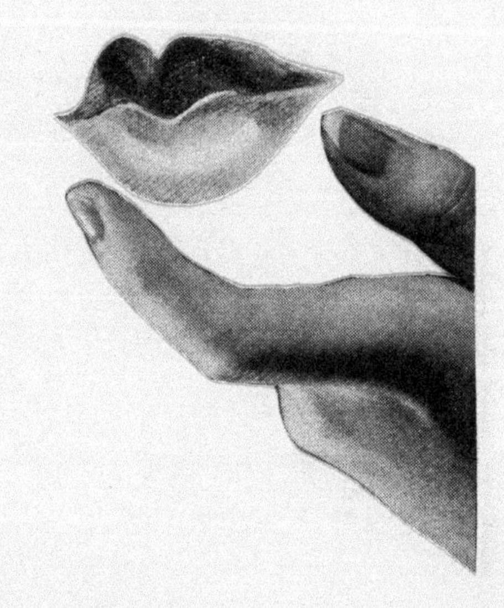

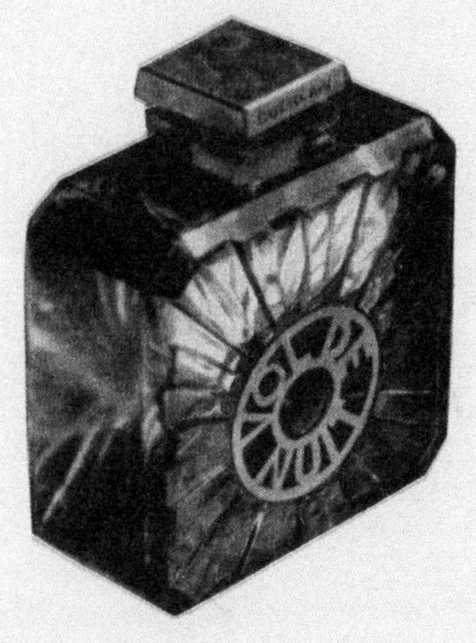

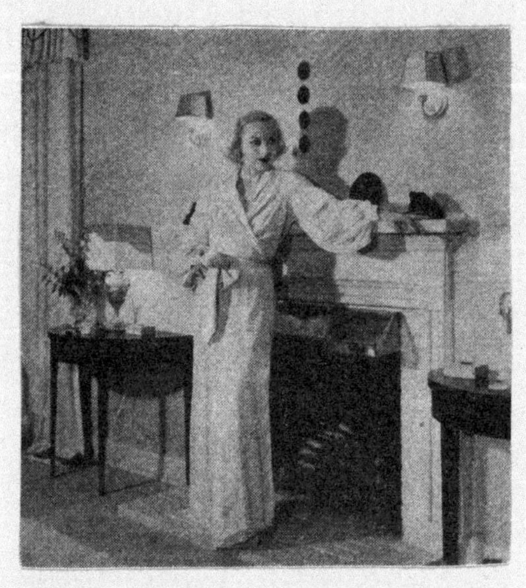

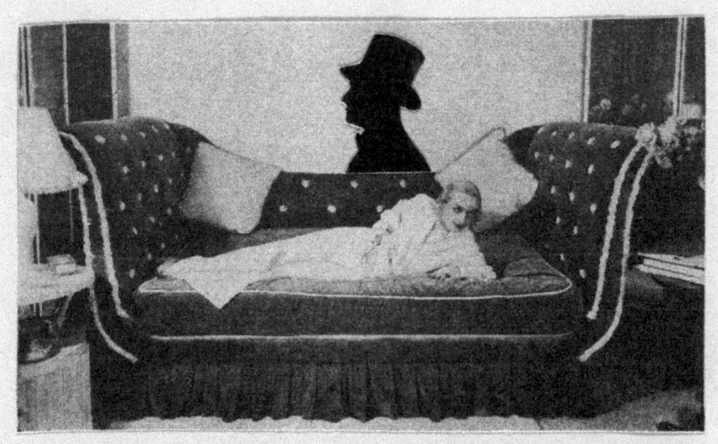

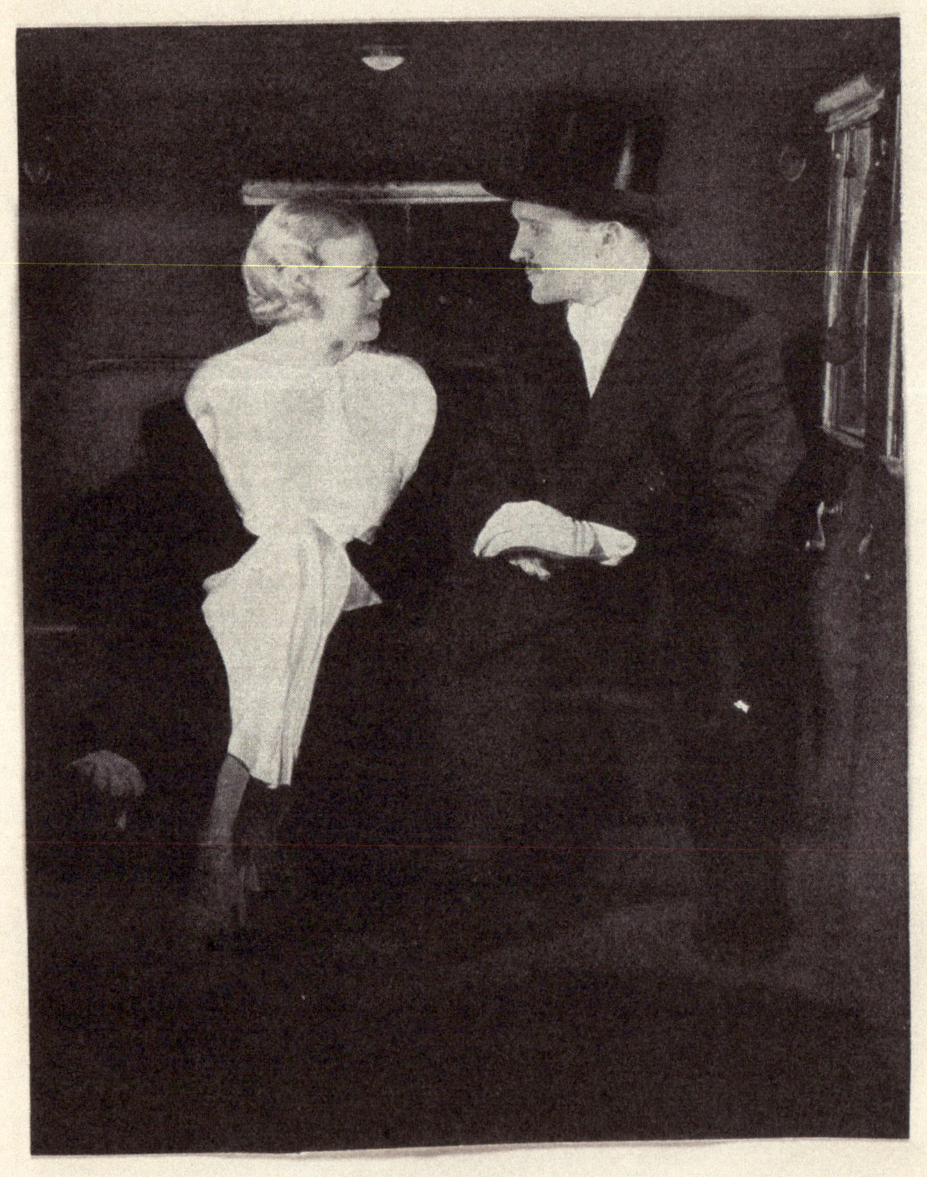

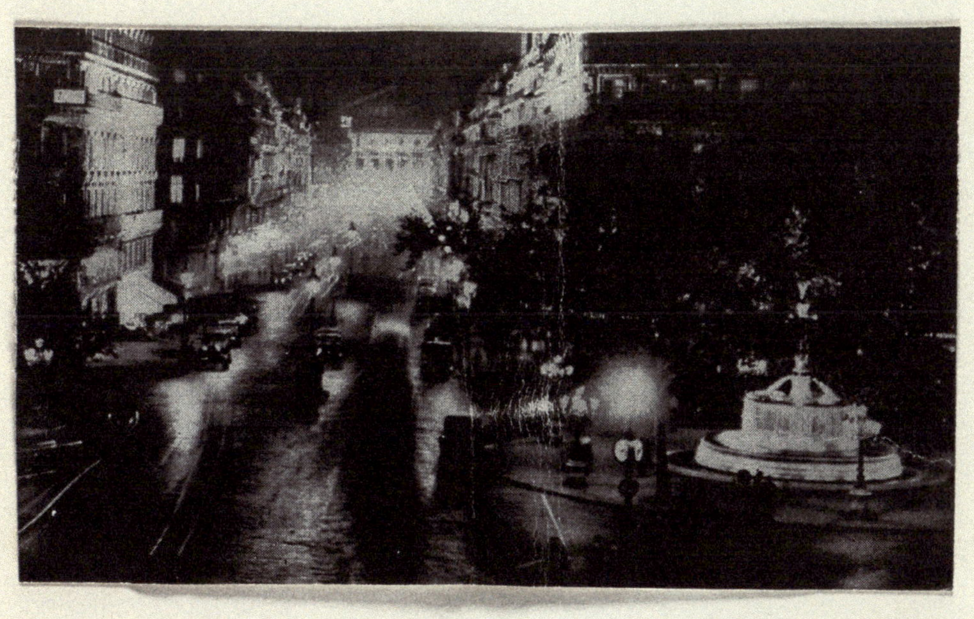

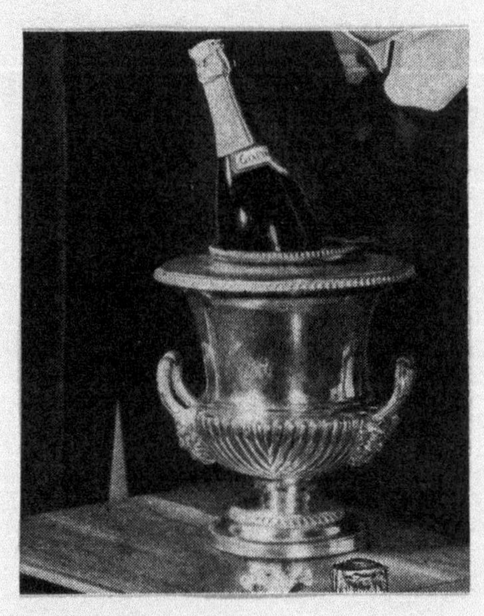

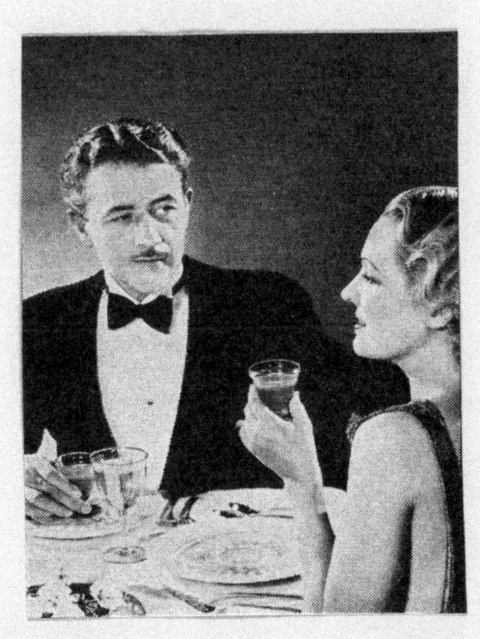

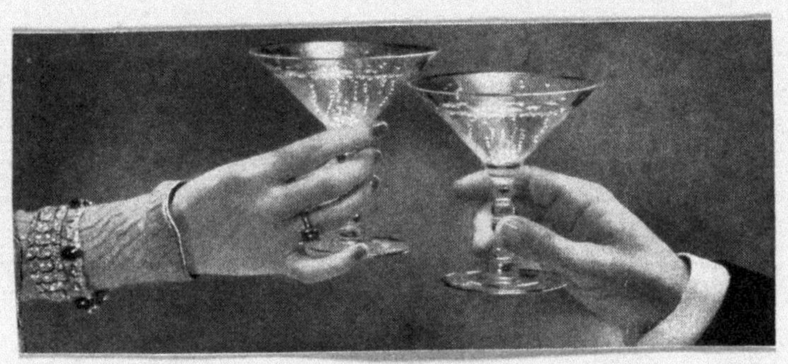

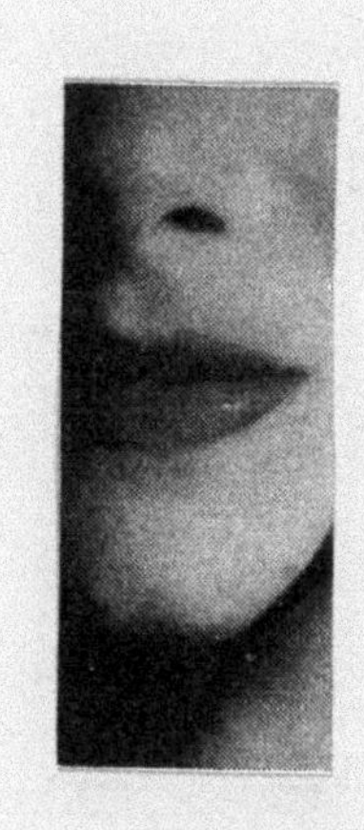

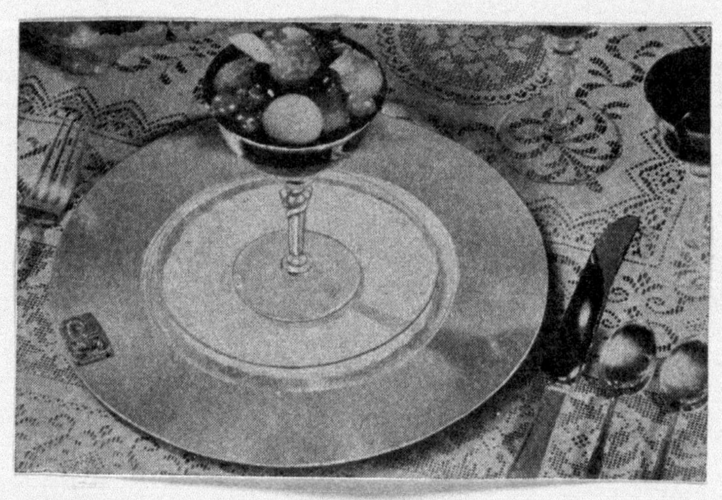

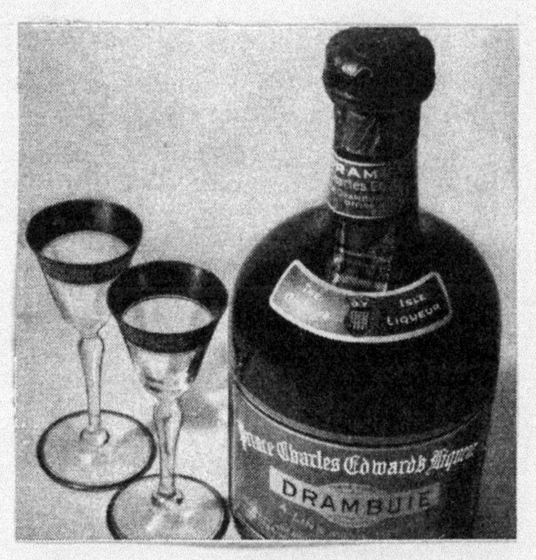
Prince Charles Edwards Liqueur
DRAMBUIE

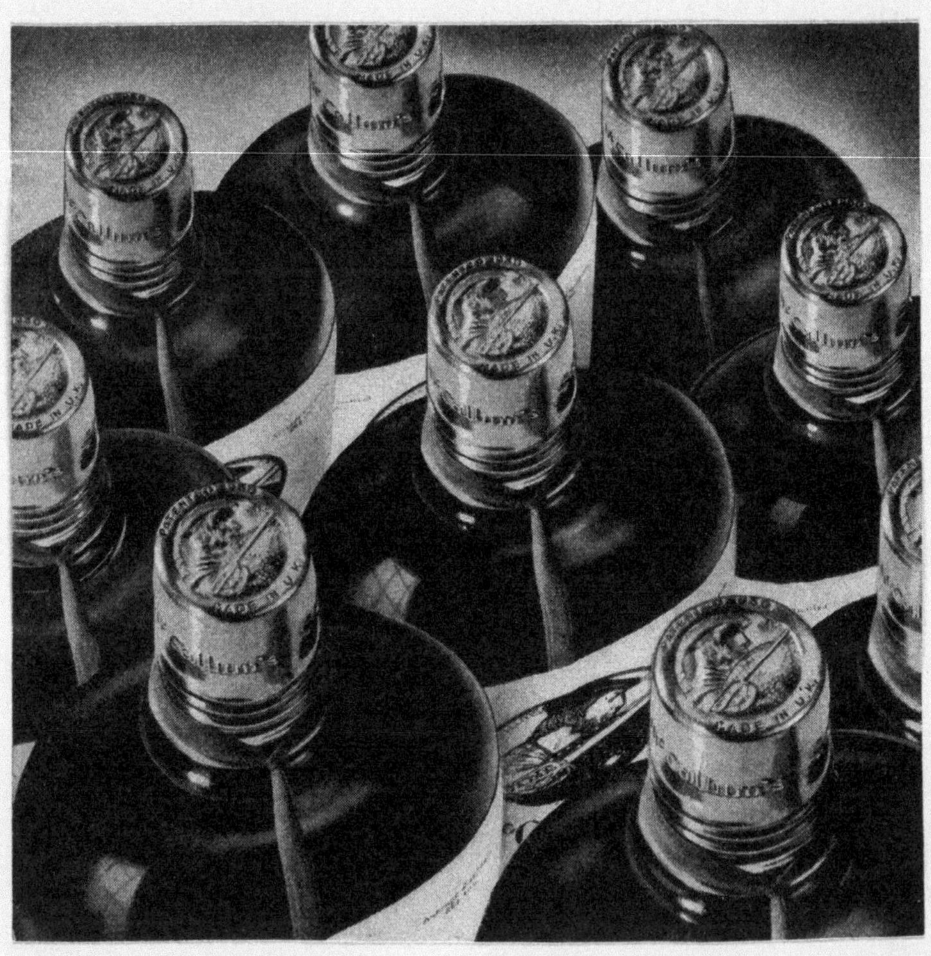

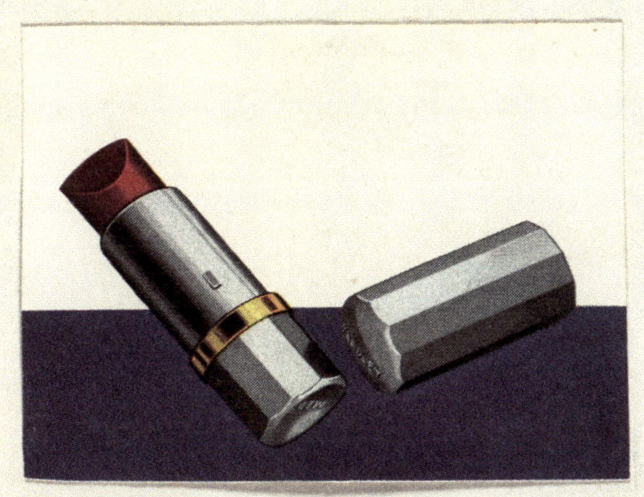

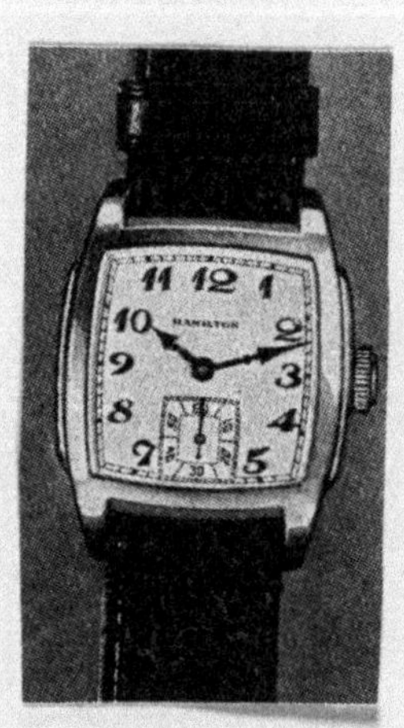

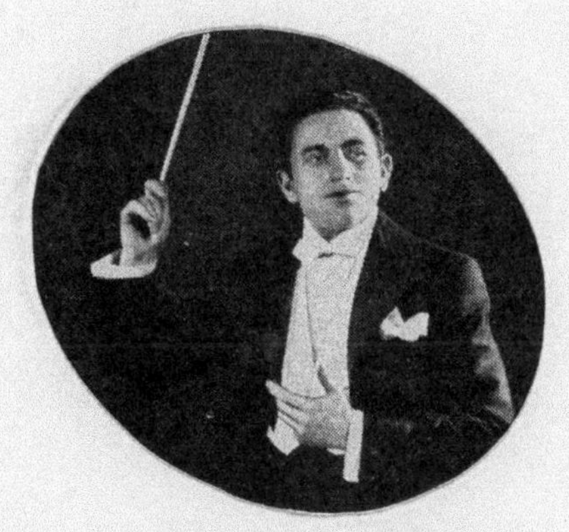

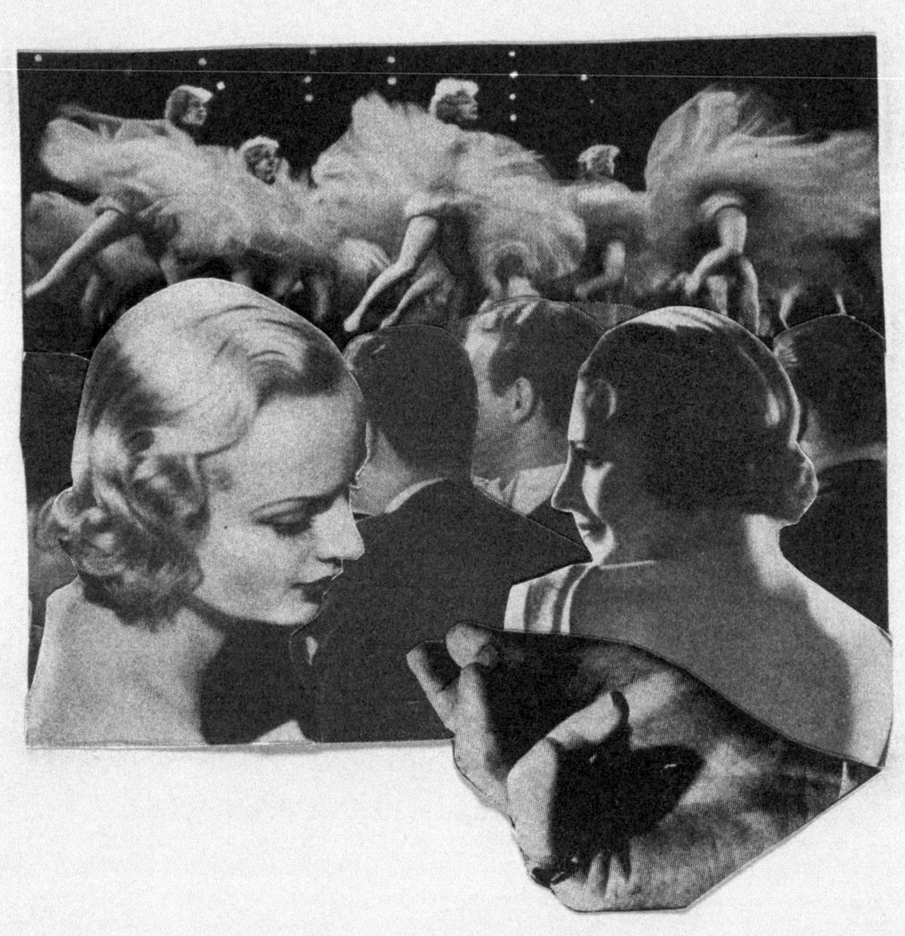

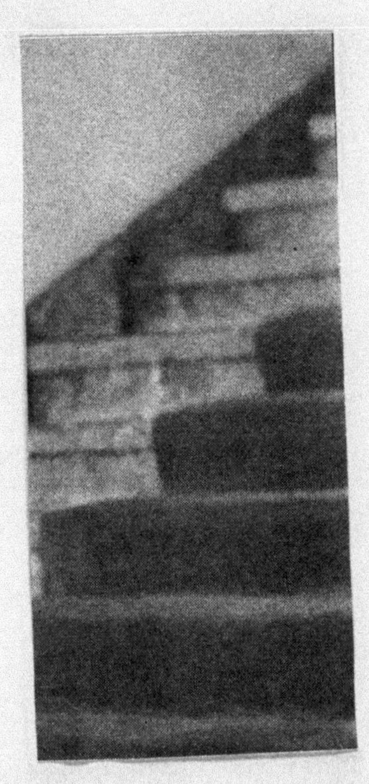

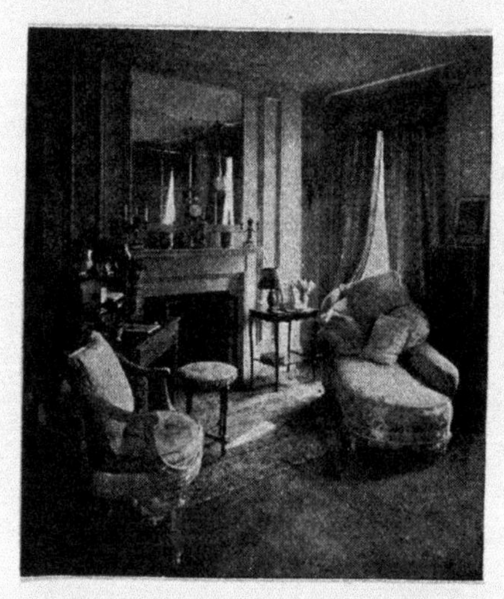

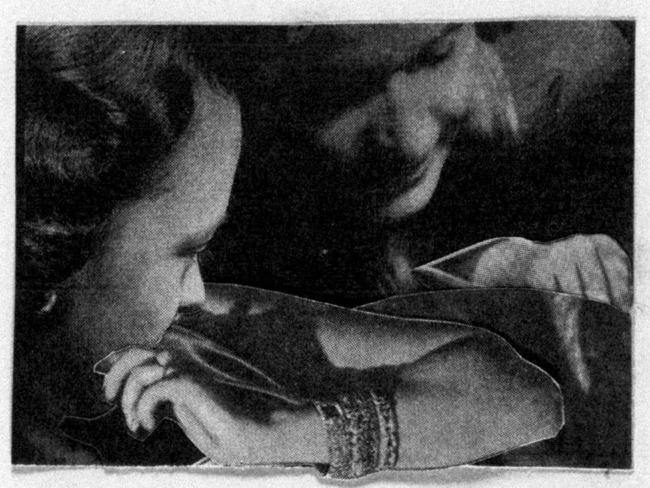

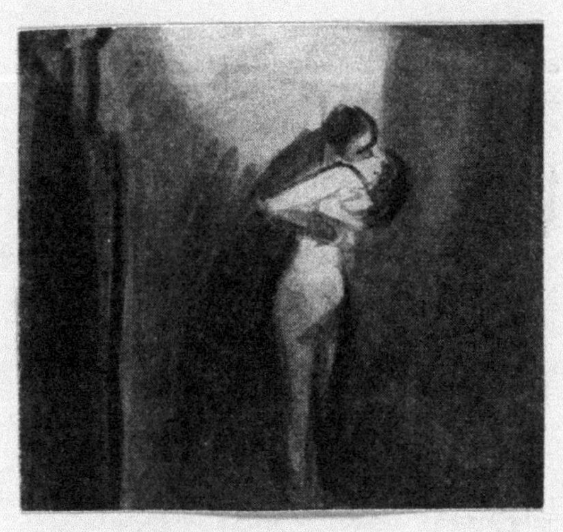

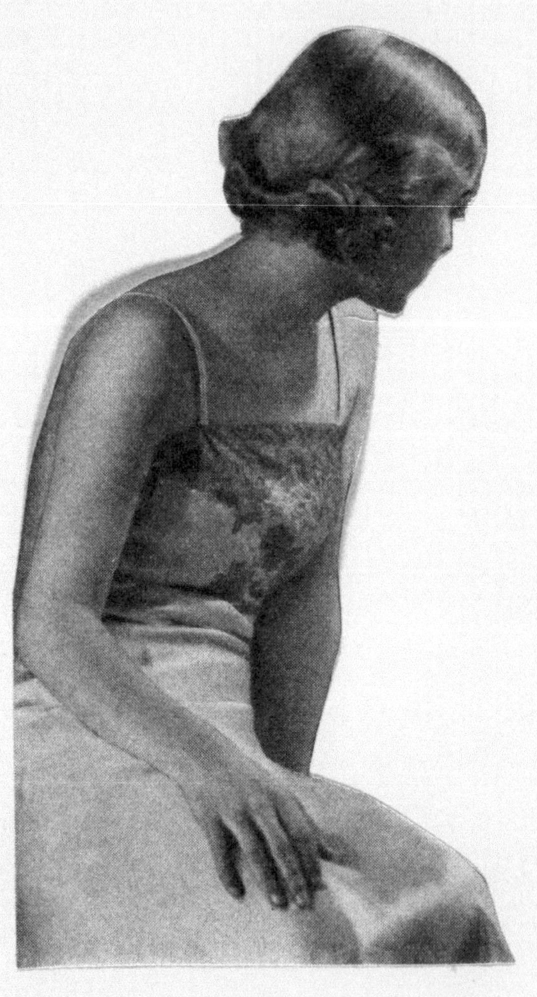

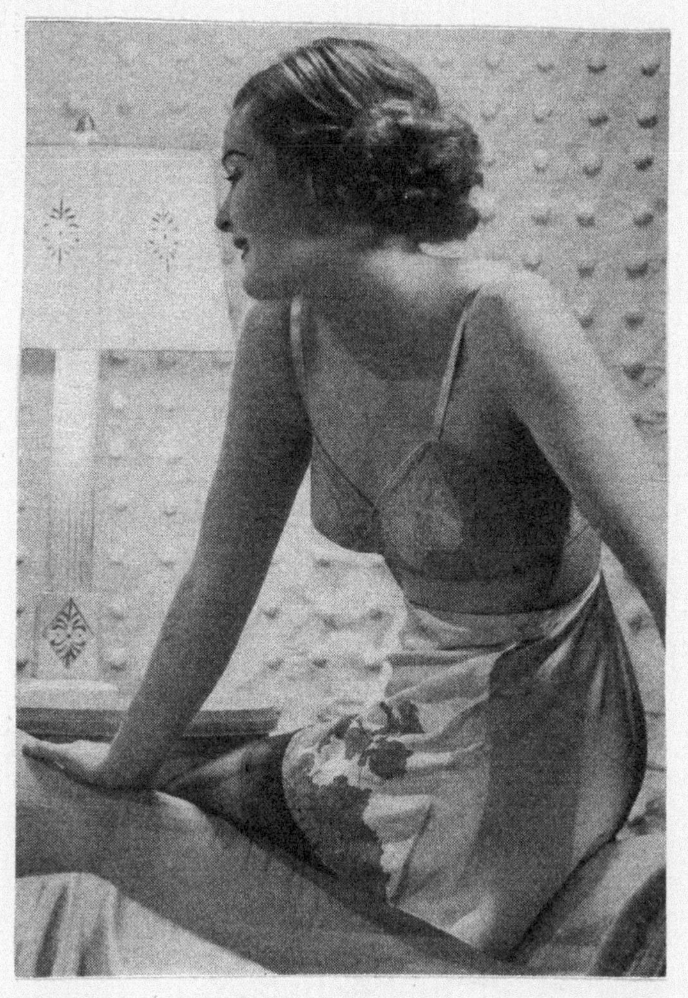

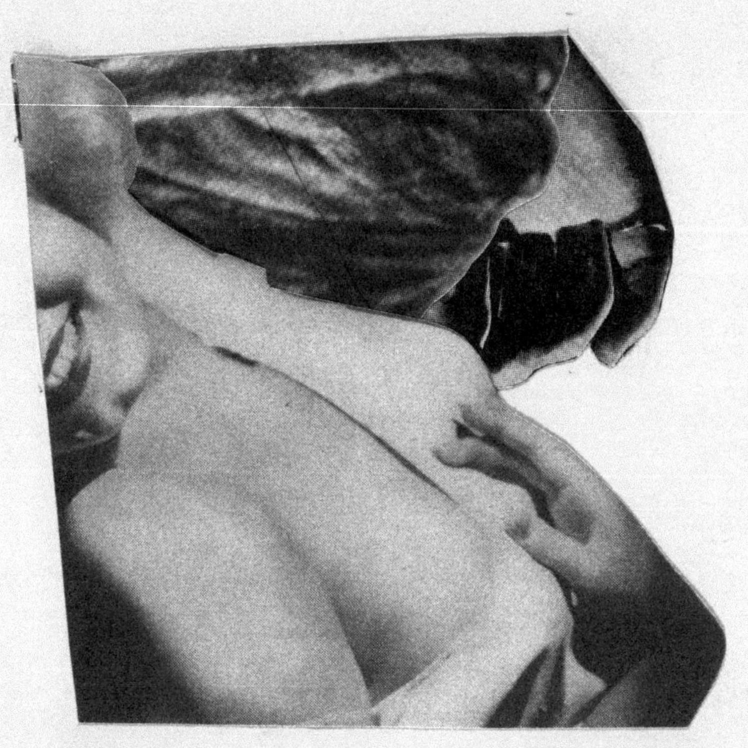

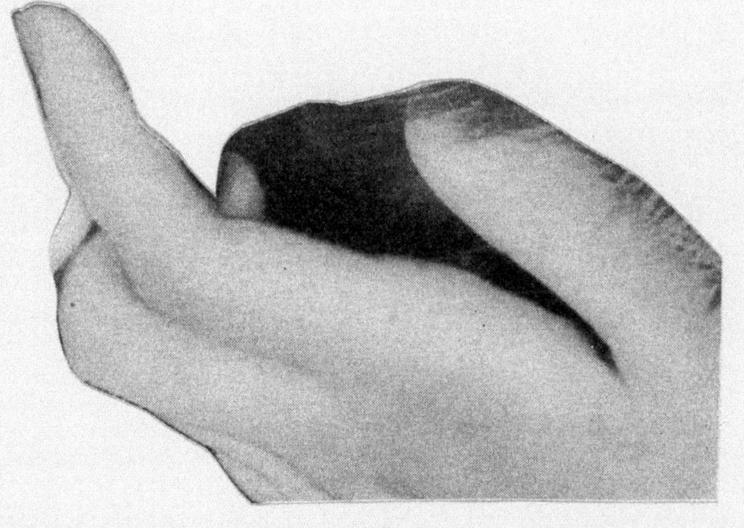

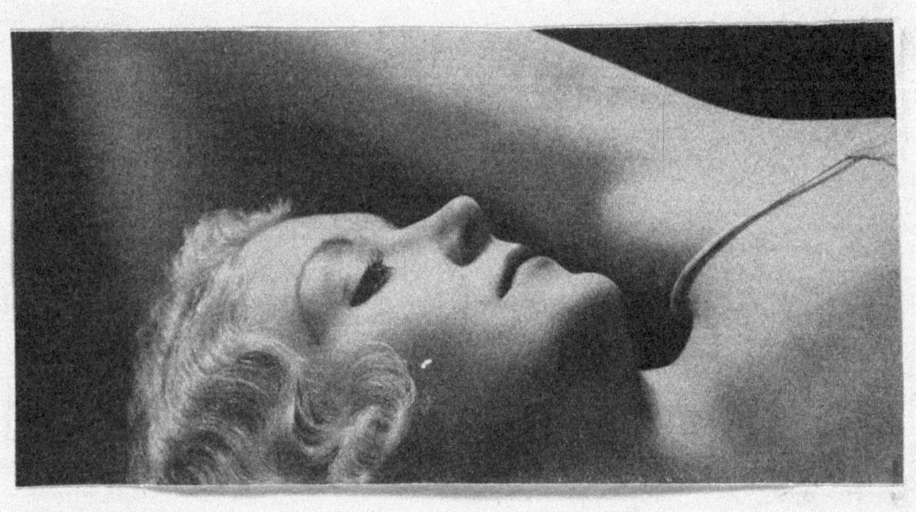

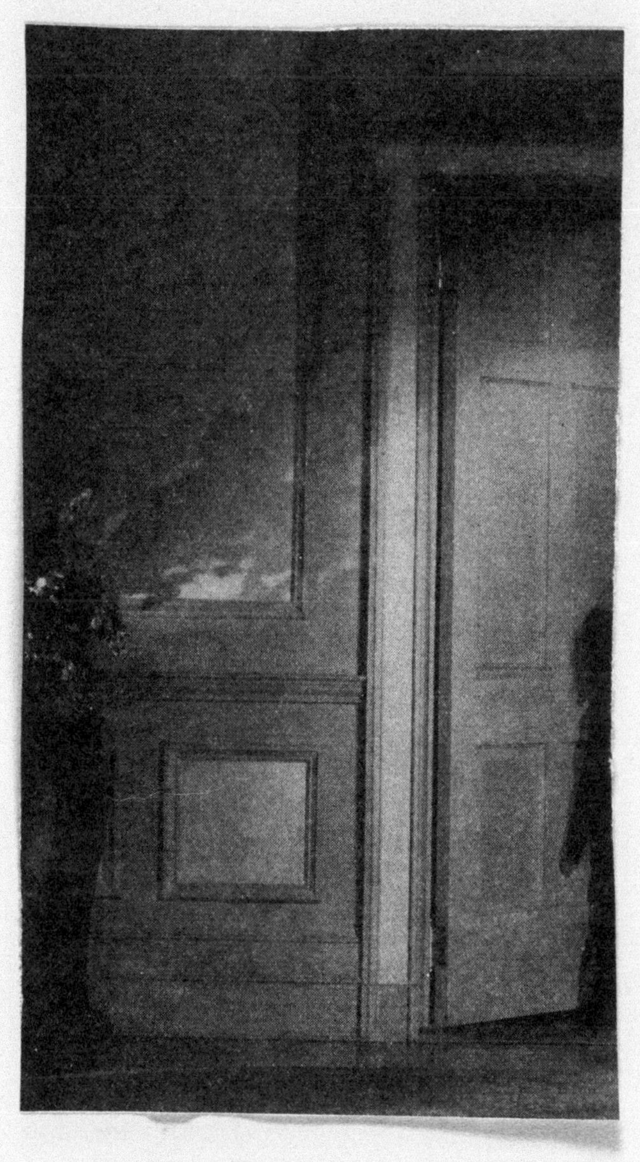

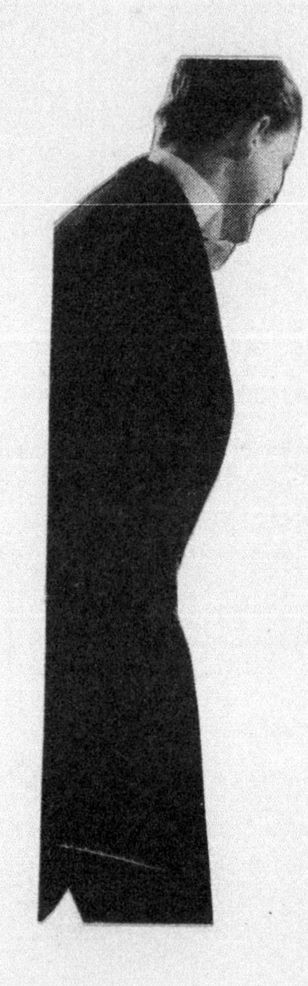

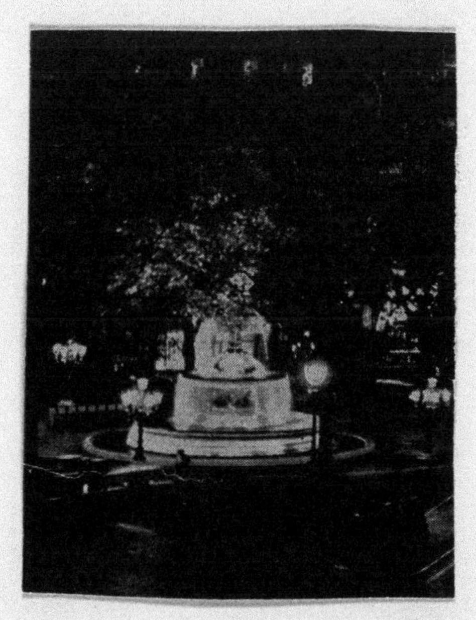

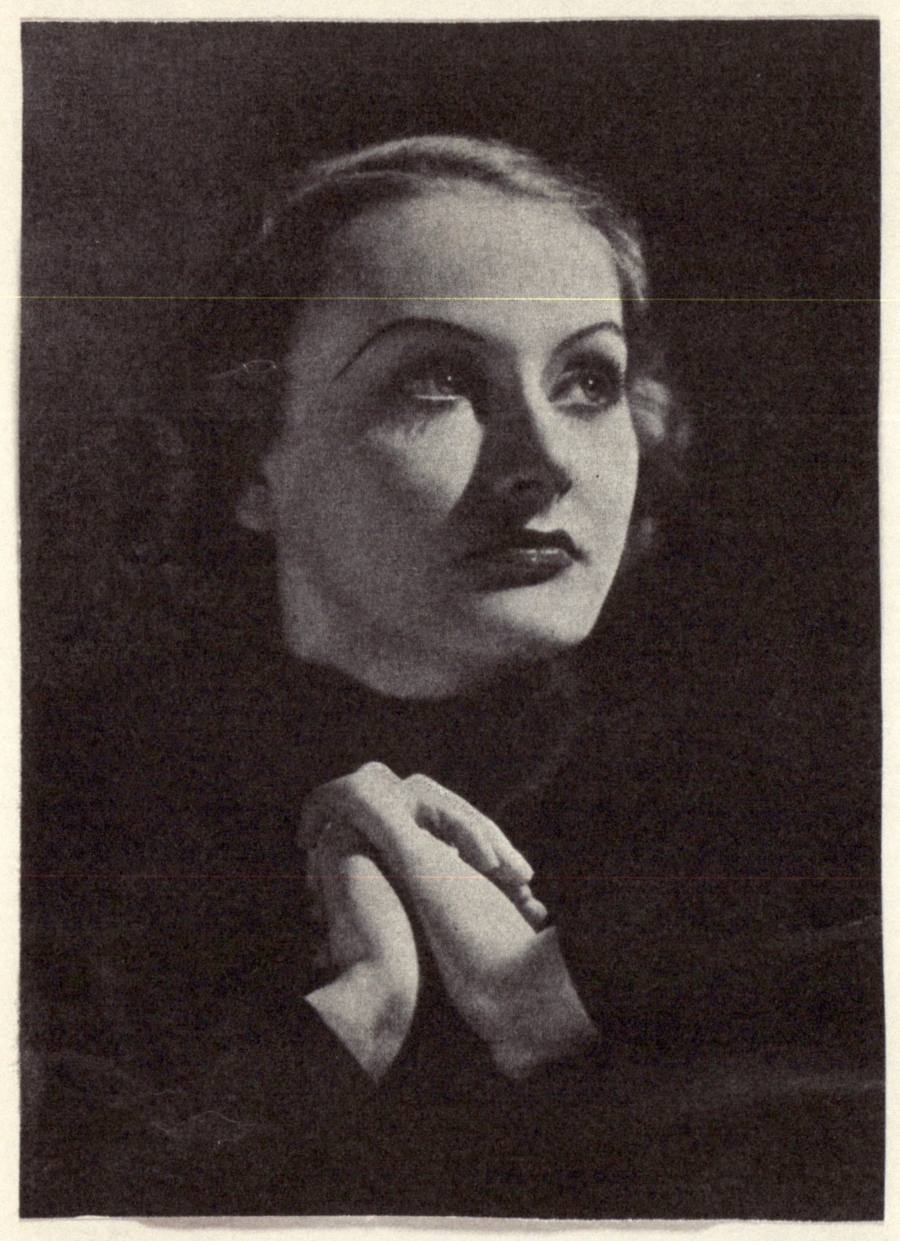

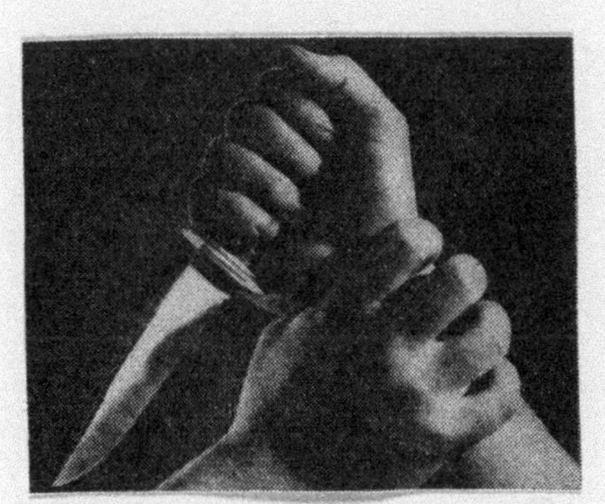

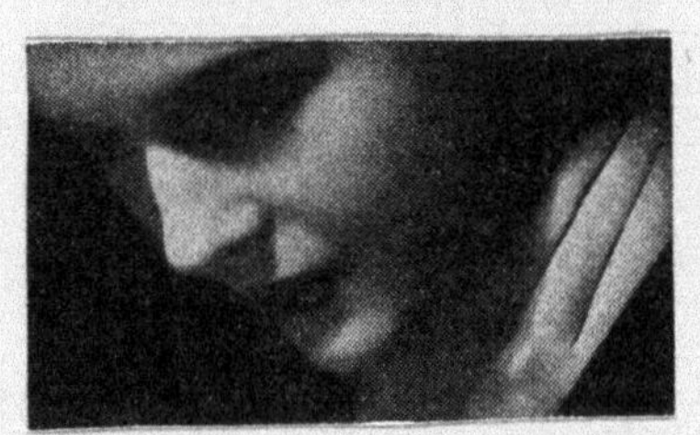

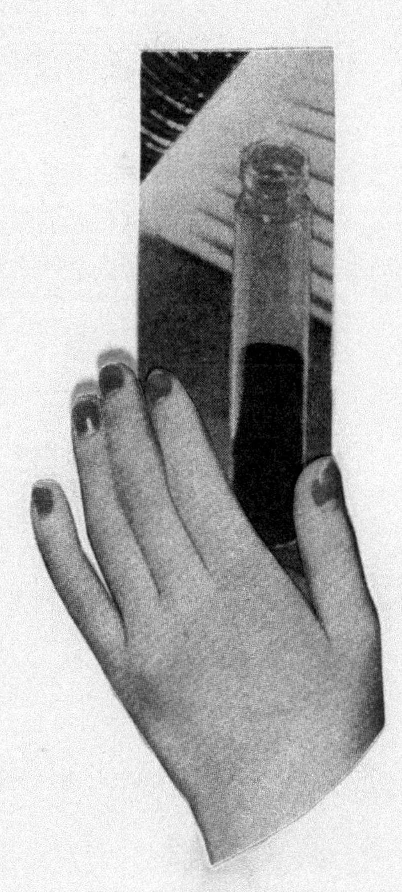

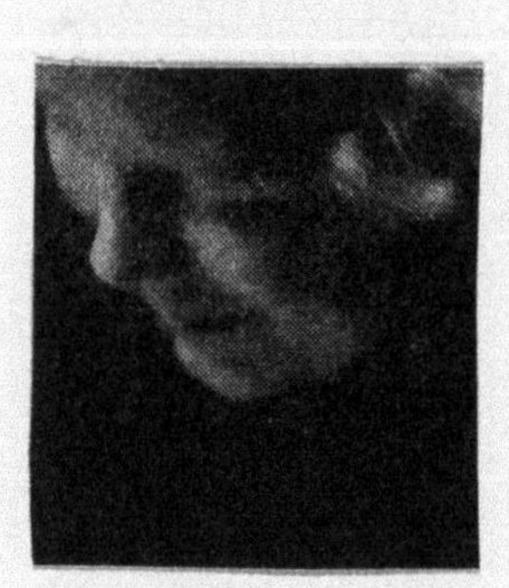

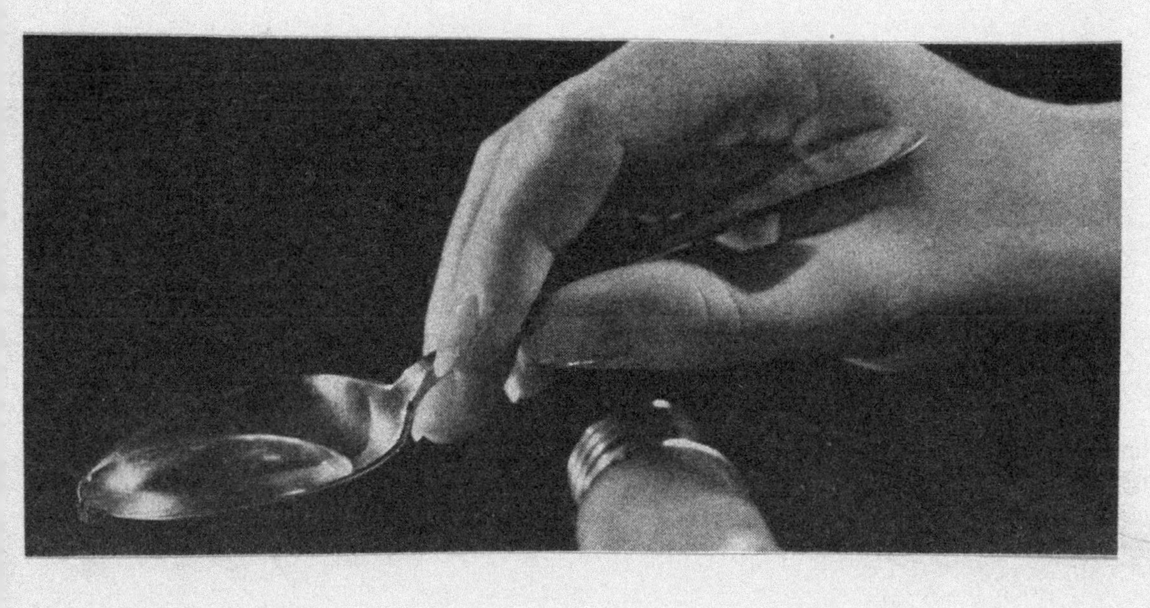

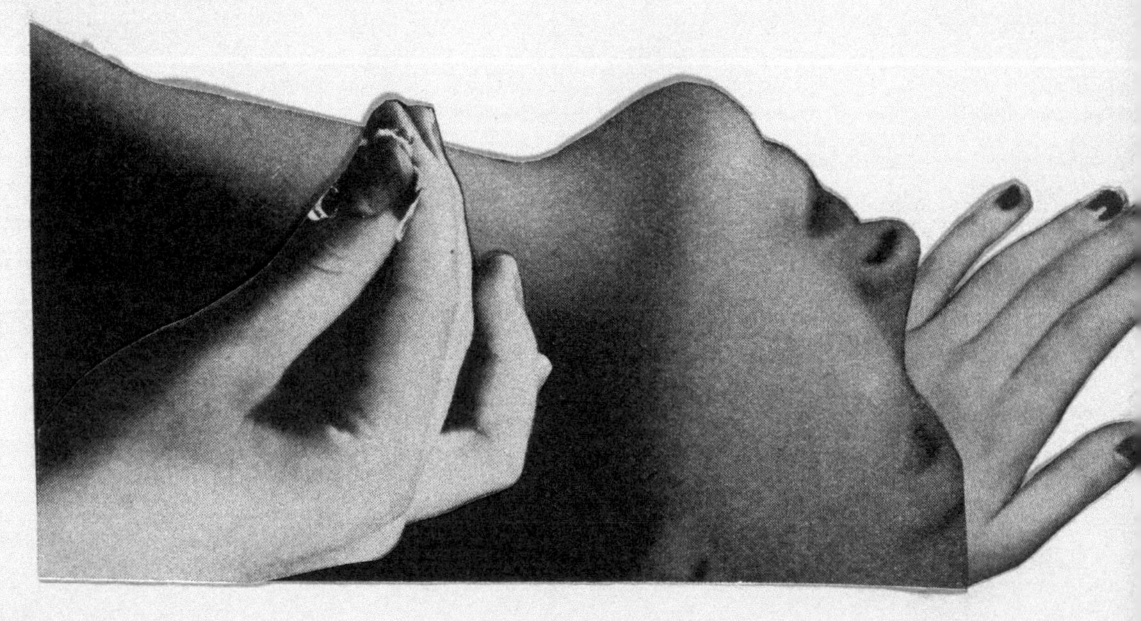

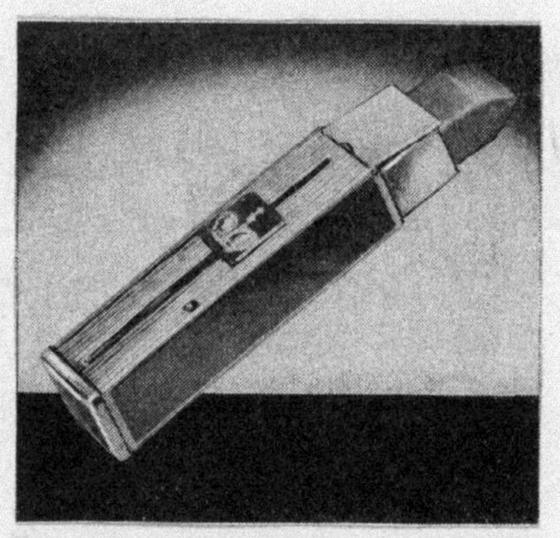

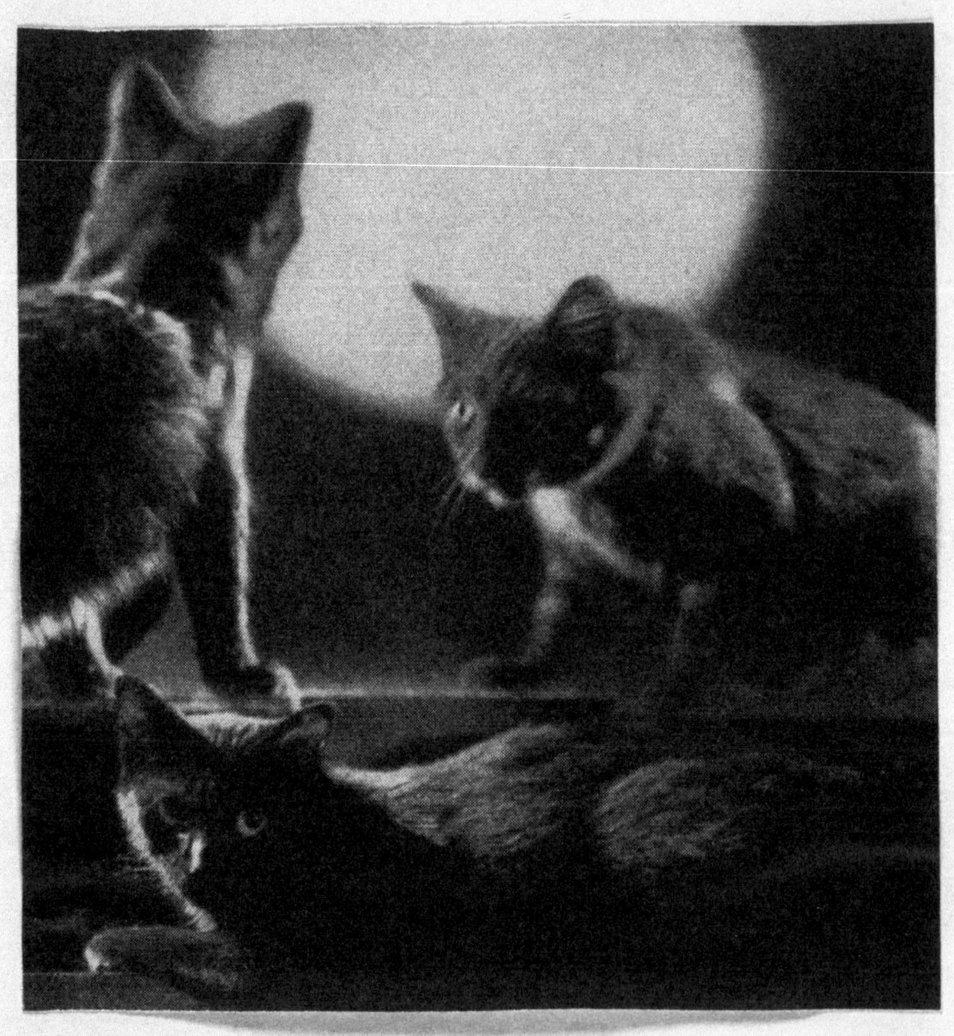

Afterword
Matthew Gale

In *Bonsoir*, Ithell Colquhoun imagined a surrealist film through a storyboard of forty-two photographs cut from popular magazines.[1] Some of these she modified by pasting them together, but the very act of extracting them from their original context allowed the sequence to elicit new meanings. It was a classic surrealist way to reimagine the world. The unstable atmosphere of the narrative is heightened by the inconsistent appearance of the characters necessarily drawn from various sources and, in selecting the imagery, Colquhoun anticipated the nature of film montage.

By choosing a salutation as her title, Colquhoun focused her story on a moment in time – a fashionably superficial evening – in which convention and ambiguity collide.[2] Her approach shares with Max Ernst's collage novels, such as *Une Semaine de bonté* 1934 ('A Week of Kindness'), a wry sense of the absurd which is exposed as emotion bursts through restraint.[3] It is in the nature of a storyboard, however, to be jagged, requiring the viewer to negotiate a series of jump cuts.[4] Colquhoun matched the liberating attitude of surrealism to a structure in which her images act, in places, like the intertitles of silent movies,[5] providing the location and the pacing for the action.

Initially, it may be difficult to grasp the storyline in *Bonsoir*. This appears deliberate. Indeed, Colquhoun may well have embraced the censors' criticism of Germaine Dulac's 1928 film *The Seashell and the Clergyman*, which was allegedly dismissed as: 'The film is meaningless; if there is meaning doubtless it is objectionable.'[6] It does become clear, however, that the evening rendezvous on which the woman embarks in *Bonsoir* is transformed when she sheds her rather formal male companion. In this respect, *Bonsoir* reflects Colquhoun's instinct to challenge gender stereotypes, also seen – especially located around the actual and mythical experience of Greece — in her erotically charged *Mediterranean* series of paintings.[7] The sexual imagery of *The Pine Family* 1940 is hardly veiled,[8] and *Scylla* 1938 offers self-exposure in tune with the publicity photographs that the artist published of herself on the beach at the time of her exhibition in June 1939.[9] *Bonsoir* displays some of these strategies, albeit embedded into the contemporary language of cinema.

The story's pacing can be measured in the three appearances of lipstick that mark the passage of time, through which Colquhoun played with the societal expectation for women to rely on their appearance.[10] They are foreshadowed by the fashionable make-up crowded on the dressing table in the second plate of *Bonsoir*, and reflect the magazine sources from which the images are clipped. The fourth plate's perfectly painted lips, framed by manicured fingers, appear to have benefitted from the preceding image of an art deco square-barrelled lipstick.[11] A little later, a close-up of a woman's mouth anticipates the seventeenth image, taken from a 1934 advertisement for the *New* Yardley lipstick.[12] This is the only colour image, and it heralds a shift in the narrative. The penultimate image of a stylish Prince Matchabelli lipstick, which indicates performance and recurrence, suggests that the story may be cyclical.[13]

Many of the images in *Bonsoir* create an atmosphere of 1930s opulent consumption. *Vol de Nuit* perfume, whose name ('night flight') reinforces the timing of the narrative, is part of the woman's preparations,[14] and the couple follow champagne with Drambuie and McCallum's Whisky. Dinner runs to twelve minutes past ten.[15] Together with the Yardley lipstick and a shot of a band leader, this is part of the pivotal moment in the storyboard, fixed in the complex image of the twentieth plate, the first in which Colquhoun's collage intervention reveals the narrative thread.

This twentieth plate is topped by showgirls observed by dinner-suited men. In the foreground, an interaction takes place — literally behind the men's backs — between two women. As they turn towards each other, this exchange is located in the hand superimposed between them, making an ambiguous gesture that lies somewhere between caressing and coercion.

While the woman on the left may be understood as the one whose evening has been followed up to that point, the woman in profile is a newcomer and brings the third element to *Bonsoir*'s triangular relationship. The gesture leads precipitously to a sensuality completely absent from the earlier formalities. The accumulations of fashion are stripped away as the narrative moves towards the languid reclining figure in the thirtieth plate. This is the core of the plot: an erotic encounter between the two women, freed from the social norms laid out in the first third of the narrative.

Inevitably, there is a denouement. Reminders of the city and the beauty of the protagonist – seen in a direct portrait photograph – precede the crisis. The jump cuts between each of the final dozen plates capture the tension precipitated by the man's reappearance. In close-ups and details that invert the tone of those used for the earlier erotic encounter, faces loom and hands struggle. Though it is not explicit, violent masculinity is set against fulfilling female sensuality. In the fortieth plate, a woman is seen in profile, arching back, her neck flanked by hands. Whether the pose is ecstatic or mortal is left unclear. The final two images – of the Matchabelli lipstick and of three cats fighting – offer the prospect of an endlessly repeating narrative of convention, seduction and confrontation.

For Colquhoun's contemporaries, used to the essentially wholesome nature of Hollywood movies, the plot twist in *Bonsoir* may have seemed most radical for its transformation of melodrama into an openly – and positive – same-sex narrative. In this, the desire encouraged by surrealism's all-consuming *amour fou* ('mad love') combined Claude Cahun's gender fluidity and André Breton's surrealist lyricism.[16] Luis Buñuel and Salvador Dalí's 1930 film *L'Age d'Or* ('Golden Age') had pitched *amour fou* as a social weapon, as Buñuel had wanted 'a moral scandal, that will consist in revolutionising the bad habits of a society in open conflict with nature.'[17] The French authorities duly banned it, although some copies evaded seizure and it was screened in London.[18] Whether Colquhoun had seen *L'Age d'Or* by the time she composed *Bonsoir* is not known, but Henry Miller's recollection of its achievement might equally be applied to her storyboard: 'The film is composed of a succession of images without sequence the significance of which must be sought for below the threshold of consciousness.'[19]

Had Colquhoun's contemporaries seen *Bonsoir*, they would have identified layers that are now less readily apparent after more than eighty years. The opening image, which locates the action in Paris, is the most easily recognised today. It is of the fountain and obelisk of the Place de la Concorde cropped from a famous photograph by Brassaï, then recently published.[20] Two other street scenes are also nocturnal, and show the twin fountains in what was then the Place du Théâtre-Française (subsequently the Place André Malraux), at the southern end of the Avenue de l'Opéra.[21] The elegance of Parisian night life is, therefore, overlaid with an awareness of the illicit and unconventional world chronicled by Brassaï.

How Colquhoun envisaged this atmosphere sitting with the most recognisable aspect of *Bonsoir* is open to speculation, for her protagonist was the Hollywood star Carole Lombard. The film actor's life, which reached the heights of success and public attention in the mid 1930s, is cannibalised in the storyboard to provide the glamour and sensuality that drives the plot. The beautiful ingénue in screwball comedies, Lombard's very public private life fed gossip columns after her divorce from actor William Powell in 1933 and her relationship and marriage with Clark Gable in 1939. It is her studio portrait that provides plate thirty-four in *Bonsoir*. Lombard's own dressing table is loaded with beauty products at the beginning, and the star herself poses at the fireplace and in the outsize chaise in the home at 7953 Hollywood Boulevard she took after her divorce (the silhouette is Colquhoun's embellishment).[22] Her companion for the evening in *Bonsoir* may be her ex-husband Powell,[23] while the twentieth image (marking the encounter with the second woman), lifts Lombard out of a well-known still from the 1932 film *No Man of Her Own* in which she is kissing Gable.[24] By cutting him away, Colquhoun focused the intensity of emotion on the gesturing hand and the newcomer – who appears to be another Hollywood star, Kay Francis. It remains unclear what Colquhoun meant by 'casting' Lombard in *Bonsoir*; although the star's fame in comedy films may suggest an under-cutting humour. It may, equally, be taken as an oblique response to the Hays Code of propriety enforced in Hollywood films in 1934; among its restrictions on sexual content was the exclusion of same-sex relationships.

As such the sensuality of *Bonsoir* challenges what one contemporary described as the 'fake morality tutored by Hays organization in Hollywood and the insane confusions and inconsistencies of the various censorship bodies'.[25] Colquhoun has cast Lombard, whose career straddled the Code, in defiance of its conservatism.

Much of the source material of *Bonsoir* derives from English-language journals of 1933–4[26] but Colquhoun's assertion that it was made in 1939 locates it at a highpoint in her engagement with surrealism. This was the summer of her solo exhibition of paintings at the Mayor Gallery, accompanied by the associated publication of her texts 'The Volcano' and 'The Echoing Bruise' in the surrealist periodical *The London Bulletin*.[27] On a visit to Paris, she met André Breton and Jacqueline Lamba and joined a group of surrealist painters revitalising an interest in automatic techniques in a château at Chemilieu that had been rented by the British painter Gordon Onslow-Ford and his sister Elizabeth.[28] Completely distinct within her practice, *Bonsoir* may fall in the moment of transition between the precision of Colquhoun's paintings shown in London and the loosening experimentation discussed in France. It does not seem to reflect the anxiety generated by the French mobilisation for war on 24 August, which would eventually precipitate the departure for the Americas of all of Colquhoun's companions at Chemilieu. Perhaps her attraction to thinking in film in the lull before the conflict reflects the view expressed in the last article published in the surrealist periodical *Minotaure*: 'it is from the limits of sleep and of dreams that film draws its source.'[29]

Notes

Introduction

1

G.R.S. Mead was a key esoteric writer and translator of the early twentieth century mainly focused on Gnostic, Eastern and Hermetic esotericism. His Quest Society, which operated in London from 1909 to 1931 or 1932 attracted the luminaries of British esotericism for lectures and debate.

2

Cut-ups are derived from a dada method proposed by Tristan Tzara of cutting lines and words from newspaper articles or other texts and rearranging them to make a new, original text. It gained a wider level of artistic currency in the 1950s with the adoption of the technique by Brion Gysin and William Burroughs.

3

Merz is a nonsense word invented by the German dada artist Kurt Schwitters to describe his collage and assemblage works based on scavenged scrap materials.

Afterword

1

Tate Archive: TGA 929/6/1. The pages are variously punched with two or four holes (suggesting re-used material). The archive catalogue entry notes that it was labelled: "Surrealism Film: BONSOIR by IC 1939". Colquhoun's note may have been written much later.

2

Surprisingly, Colquhoun tested the calligraphic appearance of her title on the reverse of plate 31. The faint pencil outline is on a larger scale, suggesting that it was traced from a lost original.

3

The structure of Max Ernst's *Une Semaine de bonté* (Paris 1934; facsimile ed. New York 1976) around days of the week make a telling precedent for *Bonsoir*.

4

In filmmaking, a jump-cut is an edit to a single, sequential shot that makes the narrative or action appear to jump forward in time.

5

An intertitle is a group of words that appear on screen as part of a film, for example dialogue during a silent film.

6

The British Board of Film Censors' response recalled in an unsigned 'Editorial: Immortalising Film', *Film Art*, vol.4, no.10 (Spring 1937), p.7.

7

The painter William Johnstone (*Points in Time: An Autobiography*, London 1980, p.236) recounted the London dealer Oliver Brown being unaware of their explicitness until pointed out by a client. Amy Hale, in *Ithell Colquhoun: Genius of the Fern-Loved Gully* (London 2020) p.61, n.15 [citing TGA 929/1/853]), notes the controversy caused by Colquhoun's male nudes when exhibited in Harrogate in 1941.

8

Victoria Ferentinou ('Ithell Colquhoun, Surrealism and the Occult', *Papers of Surrealism*, Issue 9, Summer 2011, p.12) points to the interest in androgyny shown in this painting.

9

Four images accompany Colquhoun's text 'What do I need to paint a picture?', associated with her Mayor Gallery exhibition, in *London Bulletin*, no.17 (15 June 1939), p.13. Her release of these images contrasts with the restraint of Man Ray's 1932 photographs of her; see Centre Pompidou, Dation, 1994; AM 1994-394 (3459).

10

Hale (2020, p.48) reproduces a cutting from *The Sketch* 4 June 1939 showing Colquhoun at the Mayor Gallery, the caption of which remarks on her 'picturesque checked silk house-coat' rather than her paintings.

11

This is close to, but not identical with, a 1934 Elizabeth Arden Automatic Lipstick.

12

The 1934 Yardley Lipstick encased in a steel-finished container has a brass band at the point where the cover comes off: see https://www.cosmeticsandskin.com/companies/yardley.php. Many thanks to Fiammetta Fuller Gale for this identification and that of the Matchabelli lipstick in the penultimate plate.

13

This is Prince Matchabelli lipstick (identifiable from the crown mounted on the square escutcheon); see http://www.cosmeticsandskin.com/companies/matchabelli.php. The Matchabelli showroom in New York was refurbished by Cecil Beaton in 1935 and included a painting by Pavel Tchelitchew.

14

A Guerlain perfume launched in 1933.

15

The time is shown on a 1933 Hamilton 'Scott' watch, identifiable from the 'Vintage Hamilton Watch Restoration' website [http://www.hamiltonchronicles.com/2013/01/1935-scott.html accessed 2 April 2021].

16

Claude Cahun, *Aveux non avenus*, Paris 1930, tr. in Claude Cahun, *Disavowals: Or, Cancelled Confessions*, Preface by Pierre Mac Orlan, introduction by Jennifer Mundy, afterword by François Leperlier, translated by Susan de Muth, translator's notes by Susan de Muth and Agnes Lhermitte (Cambridge, Mass. and London, 2007). André Breton, *L'Amour fou*, Paris 1937, tr. Mary Ann Caws, *Mad Love* (Lincoln, Nebraska and London 1987).

17

Luis Buñuel, interview with Andrés Ruiz Castillo, *Heraldo de Aragon*, 20 July 1930, quoted in Agustín Sánchez Vidal, '*De L'Age d'Or à La Ruée vers l'or*', in Jean-Michel Bouhours and Nathalie Schoeller, '*L'Age d'Or*: Correspondance, Luis Buñuel – Charles de Noailles, Lettres et documents (1929–1976)', *Les Cahiers du Musée national d'art moderne*, hors-série, 1993, p.19.

18

Nancy Cunard organised a London screening in January 1931. See Anne Chisholm, *Nancy Cunard* (Harmondsworth 1981), pp.218–9.

19

Henry Miller, 'The Golden Age', *The Cosmological Eye* (New York 1939 and London 1945), p.58.

20

Brassaï, *Paris de Nuit*, introduction by Paul Morand (Paris 1933).

21

Plates 9 and 33. Colquhoun's source remains untraced. A 'Tobacco map of Cuba' can be recognised through the backing sheet and running across the reverse of both clippings, confirming that they are cut from a single unidentified magazine.

22

Plates 2, 6 and 7 are Paramount Pictures publicity images used in *Motion Picture Magazine*, 1934; see http://dearmrgable.com/blog/wp-content/uploads/2011/10/zzzzzzz.jpg. The first two are from the same page, as Dorothy Manners's article 'Is Jean Harlow Hollywood's Most Underpaid Star?' (*Motion Picture*, 1933) is visible through the supporting sheet.

23

The identification of this couple remains uncertain.

24

No Man of Her Own, 1932, dir. Wesley Ruggles, Paramount Pictures.

25
Herman G. Weinberg, 'Psychopathia Cinema Sexualis', *Film Art*, vol.3, no.9, Autumn 1936, p.14.

26
The reverse of plate 40 has New York theatre listings for Yvonne Printemps in Noel Coward's *Conversation Pieces*, and for Lucienne Boyer and Vicente Escudero in *Continental Varieties*, both playing on Broadway in October 1934.

27
London Bulletin, no.17, 15 June 1939, pp.15–16, 17–18.

28
As Hale notes, the group included Yves Tanguy, Kay Sage, Esteban Francés, and Roberto and Ann Matta (see Hale 2020, pp.53–5).

29
Paul Recht, 'Cinéma-Narcisse', *Minotaure*, no. 12–13 (May 1939), p.90.

First published 2022 by order of the Tate Trustees by Tate Publishing, a
division of Tate Enterprises Ltd, Millbank, London SW1P 4RG
www.tate.org.uk/publishing

© Tate Enterprises Ltd 2022

A catalogue record for this book
is available from the British Library
ISBN 978 1 84976 8360

Distributed in the United States
and Canada by ABRAMS, New York
Library of Congress Control Number
applied for

Editor: Emilia Will
Production Manager: Roanne Marner
Picture Researcher: Emma O'Neill
Design: Design Print Bind

Colour reproduction
by Altaimage, London
Printed and bound in Italy
by Printer Trento S.r.l.

The cover for this publication is a composite of images from the original storyboard. See pp. 9, 12.

Matthew Gale was Senior Curator at Large at Tate Modern, where he was Head of Displays (2006–2021). He has curated a number of major exhibitions and with Stephanie D'Alessandro of The Met, New York, is co-curator of *Surrealism Beyond Borders*.

Amy Hale is an Atlanta-based anthropologist and folklorist writing books and essays about esoteric history, art, culture, women and Cornwall. She is the author of Ithell Colquhoun, *Genius of the Fern Loved Gully* (2020) and the editor of *Essays on Women in Western Esotericism* (2022).

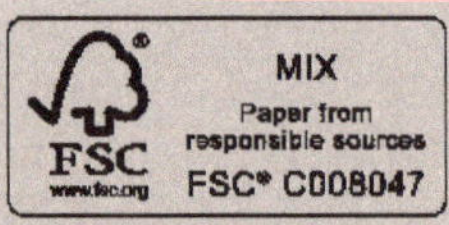